Brown and white front
wings mask bright orange
wings underneath

Butterfly uncoils
its tongue to sip
sugary nectar

Tiger moth

False eyes to
confuse
predators

Wings may look
delicate, but they
are really very
strong.

Hungry caterpillar
munching on a leaf

Butterflies
fluttering around
each other in
search of a mate

The caterpillar's
green color helps
it blend in with
the leaves.

Moth flapping
its wings very
quickly to keep
them warm

EYEWITNESS EXPLORERS

Butterflies and Moths

Written by
JOHN FELTWELL

DORLING KINDERSLEY, INC.

NEW YORK

A DORLING KINDERSLEY BOOK

Editor Jodi Block **Art editor** Vicky Wharton
Senior editor Susan McKeever **Assistant editor** Djinn von Noorden
U.S. editor Charles A. Wills **Production** Catherine Semark
Photography by Frank Greenaway **Editorial consultant** David Carter

First American Edition, 1993
2 4 6 8 10 9 7 5 3 1
Published in the United States by
Dorling Kindersley, Inc., 232 Madison Avenue, New York, New York 10016

ISBN 1-56458-227-2

Library of Congress Catalog Card Number 92-54313

Color reproduction by Colourscan, Singapore
Printed in Italy by A. Mondadori Editore, Verona

Contents

Butterflies and moths

You can spot butterflies and moths fluttering around parks, gardens, and just about anywhere that has wild flowers. Colorful flowers attract lots of butterflies, and you can watch them as they feed on nectar. Look for moths flying around streetlights at night.

Beautiful butterfly

See how many different colors you can find on the wings of a butterfly. Look at the undersides also – the colors are often completely different! You can recognize this swallowtail butterfly by the bright patches of yellow and black on its wings.

Look for swallowtails feeding on thistle flowers.

The swallowtail gets its name from the long tails on its hind wings.

Red and blue false "eyes" confuse would-be attackers

Nighttime flier

Moths are mostly nighttime fliers, but you can also spot them resting on walls, fences, and tree trunks during the day. Most moths are dull colored, but this garden tiger moth is unusually bright. Its front wings are striped just like a tiger.

The red and black colors on the tiger moth's hind wings make it easy to spot.

A closer look

A magnifying glass lets you look at butterflies, moths, and their young (caterpillars) in great detail – up to ten times bigger than they really are. If you want to pick up a caterpillar from its leaf for a closer look, be sure to use a paintbrush so you do not harm it with your fingers.

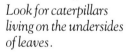

Look for caterpillars living on the undersides of leaves.

Use a notebook and colored pencils to keep a record of what you see.

Take note

When looking at butterflies and moths, it's a good idea to make sketches. Draw an outline first, then color in the different patterns. Write down where and when you made the drawing, and anything else that may help you identify the butterfly or moth.

9

Which is which?

They don't creep and crawl like beetles or ants. But butterflies and moths are insects just the same. They belong to the insect group *Lepidoptera*, which means scaly wings. Most butterflies are colorful, while moths are normally dull. Moths usually have thick, hairy bodies and feathery antennae (feelers). Butterfly antennae are long and thin.

Body parts
Like all insects, butterflies and moths have three pairs of legs, and three body parts – a head, thorax, and abdomen. They also have two large pairs of wings, antennae, and eyes.

The tip of a butterfly's antenna always ends in a club.

Head

Thorax

Eye

The wings of butterflies and moths are covered with lots of scales – like dust – which give them their color.

Abdomen

Asleep on a leaf

Most moths are small with short wings and a stubby body. When they rest, moths often slide their wings over each other into a triangular shape, so the front pair of wings covers the back wings.

Can you spot the Y-shaped mark on this silver Y moth's wings?

Front wing

Hind wing

Resting up

A resting butterfly, such as this swallowtail, claps its big wings together, straight up over its body. Look out for butterflies resting in this position on warm sunny days.

Veins on the wings work like supporting bars in a kite.

Shape and color help butterflies blend in with their natural surroundings.

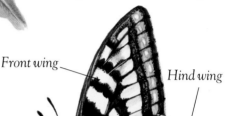

Keeping warm

Butterflies and moths have to warm themselves up before they can fly. Daytime fliers bask in the sun. Those that fly at night vibrate their wings to warm up their flight muscles.

Wondrous wings

Butterflies and moths have one thing that no other insects have – scales on their wings. Thousands of tiny scales are delicately arranged on the wings to give them color. Wings carry color-coded messages which help deter enemies and attract mates. Sometimes wings flash bright colors in the face of danger to startle predators.

Wings of lace
Some butterflies' wings are plain and brown on top. But if you catch a glimpse of the underside, you may see a beautiful lace pattern.

Look for these moths resting on willow and poplar trees.

When the moth flashes this fiery red band, it confuses predators long enough for the moth to escape.

The false eye is made up of circles of different colored scales.

Flashing color
Left undisturbed, the speckled wings of this red underwing moth blend in perfectly with the background. But when danger threatens, the moth moves its forewings forward to reveal a bright red warning color.

Hundreds of tiny scales scatter in the wind every time the moth claps its wings together.

Scale shower
The moment a butterfly or moth flaps its wings, the scales start to fall off like a shower of dust. As the insect gets older, it begins to lose the lovely colors and patterns which protect it.

If you look at the wing close-up, it's easy to see the rows of overlapping scales.

Four eyes
Many butterflies and moths send signals with their wings. The four big round marks on the peacock butterfly's wings are false eyes which scare birds and lizards away. The bright patterns and false eyes are made up of thousands of scales perfectly placed on the wing.

The colored scales fade in sunlight – so by the end of the summer this butterfly may not look so bright.

Make a butterfly

Butterfly and moth wings look very thin and fragile – but they are really quite strong. A network of veins supports the wings just like the plastic rods in a kite. You can make your own butterfly or moth kite using colorful patterns to decorate the wings. You'll need paper, scissors, glue, markers, paper straws, and string.

Chinese kites
Many Chinese butterflies have big, colorful wings. Thousands of years ago, their beauty and grace inspired expert kite-makers in China.

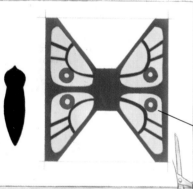

1 On a piece of ordinary paper, draw the outline and pattern of a butterfly's wings and body. Use markers to make a bright and colorful wing pattern. If you use tissue paper, the color will appear on both sides.

Make the wings about 6 inches tall with a 6 inch wingspan. The body should be 3 inches tall.

Cut two pieces of string about an inch long to make the antennae.

2 Carefully cut out the wings (keeping them joined in the middle) and the body. Then glue the body to the middle of the wings and glue the antennae to the head.

Hold the body in place and let it dry.

3 Lay a piece of string (about 18 inches long) loosely across the wings. Then place two straws over the string, and tape them down at the tips, so that they form an X.

4 Tie the string firmly around the straws and make a knot.

Fly a kite
Now you're ready to fly the kite. Just hold onto the string and run – the butterfly kite will flutter around behind you!

Vein patterns
Butterflies and moths have a special pattern of veins in their wings. This pattern helps scientists to identify them. The veins stiffen the wing and keep it in the right postition for flying.

Notice the different vein pattern in this butterfly's wing compared to the moth's wing.

Many moths have long front wings – this helps them glide with ease.

Fluttering and gliding

Depending on the shape of their wings, butterflies and moths make different patterns as they fly. If their wings are long and thin their flight is fast and straight, but if they have large wide wings they flutter around. Some butterflies, such as swallowtails, glide on currents of air – just one flap and they can sail through the sky for a long time. A frightened butterfly or moth can zoom away rapidly – up to 600 flaps a minute and over 30 miles per hour!

Light landing
Holding its wings out wide like a parachute, a butterfly gently drops before landing on its legs.

The female flaps her wings quickly, trying to avoid the male below.

As the male lifts its wings, they push air backward, so that the butterfly moves forward.

Loop the loop
If you take a walk through a forest glade and see one butterfly looping around another, you may have spotted a pair of silver-washed fritillaries. The male flies below the female to pass his scents under her antennae. These scents will eventually persuade the female to mate with him.

Speedy flight

The wings of a jet fighter plane look just like those of a moth. Both have long thin wings that point backward for speedy flight. This death's head hawkmoth is one of the fastest-flying moths in the world.

The next wing beat will pull the male down below the female once again. He repeats this about four times.

When the wings come down, the butterfly moves upward.

The butterflies do not do much damage during the fight, and when it's over, the first butterfly returns to its place in the sun.

After a while the intruding butterfly gives up the spiral game and flies off to find another sunny spot.

Fight for light

The speckled wood butterfly likes to bask in a sunny spot on the woodland floor. If another butterfly tries to take over this spot, the two fly around and around, bumping into each other many times. The fight does not last long, and the spot's original "owner" usually wins the spiral battle.

Eyes and seeing

Instead of having just two eyes, butterflies and moths have thousands! Each large eye, called a compound eye, is made up of lots of tiny eyes. Each tiny eye sees what is straight ahead – and when the insect looks at an object, it sees lots of little objects at once.

Eyes look out for danger

This is how an insect sees you through a few of its eyes.

Tiny eyes

The tiny eyes are called ommatidia (*om-a-tid-ee-a*). Each eye forms a small picture. The insect's brain then puts all the pictures together.

Huge eyes

Huge compound eyes allow insects to see all around. Try creeping up on a butterfly – you'll be surprised at how quickly it spots you and flies away.

Each tiny ommatidium has a clear surface which lets in light.

✋ *Don't touch light bulbs – they can get very hot.*

Pseudopupil

Spotty eyes
When they are alive, butterflies and moths often have a dark pattern of little spots, called pseudopupils (*sudo-pupils*), on their eyes. No one knows exactly why they are there. When the insect dies, the pseudopupils fade.

Bright lights, big risk
Look for nighttime moths fluttering around windows and streetlights. Moths are attracted to the light, but become an easy target for bats which swoop around the bulb, snapping up the easy meal.

Only insects can see these lines.

Invisible guides
The light from the sun that comes after purple on the rainbow is called ultraviolet light. We cannot see this light, but butterflies and moths can. Some flowers, such as this lesser celandine, have ultraviolet guides on their petals – insects use these guides like a runway to guide them to the tasty nectar.

Smelling and sipping

They may not have a nose like we do, but butterflies and moths have an amazing sense of smell. They use their antennae to detect scents – sometimes as far as two miles away. Most butterflies and moths have a long tongue called a proboscis that they use for sipping sweet nectar and other liquids. Look for them fluttering around flowers as they feed.

Smell detectors
Butterflies need huge antennae to detect flowers and to find other butterflies. Each antenna has thousands of tiny holes that absorb smells.

A butterfly keeps its proboscis rolled up like a spring until it is ready to feed.

Long straws
A butterfly's tongue is just like a straw. But it has to uncoil it in order to get to the sweet liquids that lie at the bottom of flowers.

The antennae are divided into segments.

Having a drink
Butterflies drink in all sorts of funny places. You may spot one at the edge of a puddle, at an animal's droppings, or in the mud. This butterfly is drinking some sweet sap oozing from a log.

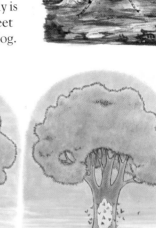

Attracting moths
The sweet smell of sugar attracts moths. You can see this for yourself by coating a tree trunk or fence with a sugary mixture. Use some old syrup or honey mixed with a little bit of water to make a thick, gooey mess.

1 With a paintbrush, brush this mixture onto a tree trunk at dusk on a warm summer night.

2 Using a torch, check for moths every half hour. Thieving ants and beetles will come to visit too.

Extra long tongue
The tongue of this Darwin's hawkmoth is incredibly long, even longer than its body. But it fits neatly into this flower, where it sucks up sugary liquids.

Hidden nectar

The scientist Charles Darwin thought there must be a flower with an extra-long tube to hold the moth's proboscis – and he was right!

Looking at legs

Like all insects, butterflies and moths have three pairs of legs, which are attached to the thorax. Each leg is divided into four different sections, all hinged together for easy movement. They use their legs for walking and for landing on leaves and flowers. Once they've landed, they use their feet to taste the leaves.

Look for this moth resting on tree trunks during the day.

When at rest, this moth keeps its legs perfectly still and fools birds into thinking it is a dead leaf.

Muscular femur (thigh)

Hinge joint

Spiky spines

This eyed hawkmoth has tiny backward-facing spines on the lower part of its six legs. They dig in if an enemy attacks.

The tibia (lower leg) has lots of hairs and spines.

Leg shell

Look for three pairs of legs at the front of a caterpillar's body. These become the true legs of the adult butterfly or moth. The adult's leg muscles are on the inside of a tough protective shell called an exoskeleton. The leg ends in a claw for gripping twigs.

Happy landing

Moths use all six of their legs when they come in for a landing. But about half the world's butterflies land on only four legs. The other, weaker pair is tucked under the insect's head.

Front legs look like little brushes.

Its four legs are spread out for landing.

This brown butterfly has six legs, but only four are strong enough to land on.

Keeping clean

Moths have to keep their antennae in very good condition in order to detect smells. This moth is using its leg to clean its antennae. Each antenna has lots of little shelves that collect pollen from flowers as the moth feeds. The stiff spines and hairs on the leg work just like a comb to remove the pollen.

The butterfly also uses her antennae to check the plant's smell.

Taste test

Many butterflies and moths have special cells on the tips of their feet that they use for tasting leaves. They only need to touch down for a few seconds to identify the plant. If the leaf passes the taste test, they can lay their eggs on it.

23

Getting together

Have you ever noticed a pair of butterflies or moths flying in circles around one another? Flying like this allows them to smell each other. By smelling special body scents called pheromones (*fer-o-mones*), they can identify a mate of the right species. If the smell is right, the couple will mate. Finding the right mate is called courting.

In hot climates, mud-puddling is a common sight.

Pheromones are usually present in tiny scent scales on wings.

Mud-puddling
Male butterflies gather on riverbanks to drink water which is rich in mineral salts. These salts help butterflies make special smells to attract a mate.

Some male moths have large, feathery antennae that can smell a female up to three miles away!

I'm over here!
Male moths release smells by putting out pencil hairs from their bodies. These hairs scatter the pheromones on the breeze, where females will smell them.

24

The male butterfly has a pair of claspers that encloses the female's rear end.

Joined together

These butterflies are mating. They will stay like this, out of danger in the bushes, for about an hour. Afterward, the male flies away and the female lays her eggs.

This female's wings have special colors and patterns to attract male butterflies.

Dancing in the sky

Keep an eye out for butterflies or moths dancing and fluttering around each other on warm summer days. A courting couple may fly together for over an hour.

All about eggs

Butterfly and moth eggs come in many shapes and sizes, but they are all the first stage in an insect's life. The female lays her eggs on or near the right plant that will be food for the caterpillar when it hatches. This plant is known as the food plant.

The cycle of life

Butterflies and moths pass through four stages during their lives. They begin as eggs and then hatch into caterpillars. When fully grown, the caterpillars form a pupa which produces an adult. These changes are called metamorphosis.

Laying eggs

As this female silver silk moth lays her eggs, she glues them to the stem so that they do not fall off. Sometimes she produces special hairs to put on the eggs to protect them from ants.

The moth curls her abdomen round to put each egg in place.

Egg plant

This African moth disguises her eggs by gluing them in a ring around a twig. Other insects and spiders are tricked into thinking that they are just part of the plant.

This little group of eggs will hatch into tiny caterpillars and start to nibble on the leaf.

Egg hunt

Search for groups of eggs on leaves, twigs, and buds. They are usually on the underside of leaves, and their color may blend in with the leaf – so look carefully.

The female marbled white butterfly flies low over the grass so that her eggs will hit their grassy target. She releases the eggs from her abdomen.

Egg identity

Some butterflies and moths lay more than 1,000 eggs, all together. But the red admiral butterfly lays her eggs singly, on nettle leaves. You can identify a red admiral egg by the seven little ridges around the edge.

Falling eggs

A few kinds of butterflies drop their eggs over the grass as they fly along. Wherever the eggs fall, they stick. Luckily, the caterpillars that hatch like to eat grass!

Caterpillar birth

Being born is a dangerous start to a caterpillar's life. It has only a few minutes to emerge from the egg and hide from hungry predators. Once it is safely hidden, it begins a life of nonstop eating. If the caterpillar is lucky, it will live for about a month before it becomes a butterfly.

Eggs with a sting
Look for the red admiral near stinging nettles. It lays single eggs on the top of the nettle leaves.

Ready to go
At first, the pale green egg is full of liquid that looks a bit like soup. A tiny caterpillar is growing inside the liquid. After about seven days, the egg becomes very dark – it is now ready to hatch.

Ribbed surface helps the egg keep its shape.

Caterpillar body curled up inside egg

Opening the egg
The tiny caterpillar already has tough jaws. It munches a circle around the top of the egg and then it rests for awhile. You can see the hairy black head poking out of the top.

The old egg case is now transparent. Can you see the supporting ribs on both sides?

The leaf contains minerals the caterpillar needs to grow and eventually become an adult butterfly.

Out in the open

Curled up tightly for so long, the new caterpillar now pulls itself out of the egg like a jack-in-the-box. It stretches out in the open for the first time.

Green screen

As soon as it hatches, the caterpillar pulls the sides of the leaf together with silk threads. This shelter keeps it hidden from predators. Tucked away behind the leafy screen, the hungry caterpillar eats its first nettle-leaf meal.

Camping caterpillar

Look for leaf tents in gardens – you may find a red admiral caterpillar inside! The caterpillar spends its whole life hidden in the tent. During this time, it changes its skin four times to get bigger.

Clever caterpillars

Birds, lizards, and mammals love the taste of caterpillars. So caterpillars have developed plenty of ways to keep these enemies away. Some disguise themselves as snakes, or show off a pair of big scary eyes. Other caterpillars can blast a nasty-smelling spray into the face of hungry predators.

Small snake?
By puffing up the front of its body and showing off its false eyes, this caterpillar tricks birds into thinking it's a small snake.

Stand straight
When disturbed, these caterpillars flick their bodies into the air. If they all do it together and quickly, it suprises birds and lizards.

Zebra with horns
If you thought only large animals have horns, then look again – the head horns and long spiny hairs on this zebra caterpillar warn predators that an attack might be painful.

Simple eyes at the side of their head allow caterpillars to make out light and dark.

Tail

✋ *Be careful – this caterpillar can spit acid in an enemy's face.*

Inchworms move along inch by inch – often quickly to avoid danger.

Eyespots

Fierce face
When danger threatens, the puss moth caterpillar flashes the bright red markings on its face and swings its tail in the air.

Inching along
These caterpillars are also called loopers because of the way they move. They hold on with their back legs and move the front end as far away as possible. Then they bring the rear end up to the front so that it forms a loop. Look for inchworms on twigs and leaves in the spring.

Lobster disguise
It is easy to recognize the caterpillar of a lobster moth. When threatened by a predator, it raises its head and tail in the air and looks just like a little lobster.

Poisonous spiky horns keep enemies away

Blending in

Caterpillars can look invisible when they pretend to be something else. By copying the color of the food they are eating, or by looking like twigs or bird droppings, some caterpillars fool their enemies into thinking that they aren't really there. When something blends into the background like this, it is called camouflage.

Breaking up

You can see how the lines on this caterpillar help to break up its outline. Blending in with the leaves allows the insect to feed in peace.

Look for hawkmoth caterpillars feeding on leaves in the summer.

Is it or isn't it?

This shiny black swallowtail caterpillar looks exactly like a bird dropping. Now imagine you are a hungry bird – would you risk a bite?

Twiggy disguise
Peppered moth caterpillars look like twigs. They have no middle legs and are the same shape and color as the twigs.

Little and large
Poisonous large white caterpillars don't need to hide, because enemies know to keep away. Tasty small white caterpillars, however, are camouflaged to stay alive.

At first, small white caterpillars feed unseen in the center of the cabbage.

Mix and match
Caterpillars aren't born green – they turn green! They mix the yellow colors from leaves with their own blue colors, which they use to digest food.

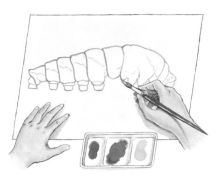

Paint a caterpillar outline and fill it in with yellow paint. Then add some blue paint. What color is your caterpillar now?

Invisible owls
Packed together by the stem of their banana leaf food, these owl butterfly caterpillars are almost invisible – and safe from hungry hunters.

Caterpillars lie lengthways to blend in with the stem.

Feeding machines

Have you have ever watched a caterpillar munch away non-stop on a leaf? If so, you may not be surprised to learn that it can increase its body weight at least one hundred times in just a few weeks. The tiny caterpillar begins eating as soon as it hatches from an egg.

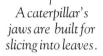

A caterpillar's jaws are built for slicing into leaves.

The meal begins
The caterpillar grasps the leaf between its legs and starts to eat. Caterpillars are always hungry. The more the caterpillar eats, the more it grows.

Caterpillar disguises itself as a leaf to fool its enemies.

The caterpillar stretches out its head and chews down towards its body.

Halfway there
Having finished one leaf, the caterpillar moves on to another. It eats the softer, juicier parts first.

All finished

The caterpillar has now nearly finished the third leaf. It will move on to another shoot if there are not enough leaves left on this one.

Nothing is safe

Caterpillars don't find their food only in the garden. Some moth caterpillars eat wood, some dine on cotton, and others eat house dust. Some even nibble feathers!

Make your own caterpillar restaurant

You can study caterpillars eating in their natural habitat by "sleeving" a low branch of their food plant. You will need a piece of muslin or net, needle and thread, string, and scissors for this project.

Ask an adult for help when using scissors.

1 Sew the longest edges of a rectangular piece of muslin together to make a tube.

2 Find a branch that has feeding caterpillars on it and carefully slip the muslin tube over it. Tie the tube at both ends.

3 Check how much the caterpillars eat and grow each day. Move them to a new branch of the right food plant when they finish these leaves.

Changing skin

Butterflies and moths go through four stages in their lives. The third stage is the pupa – also called the chrysalis (*kris-a-lis*). This is when a caterpillar changes into an adult. As a caterpillar grows, it changes its skin four or five times. When it has eaten enough, it outgrows its skin for the last time and turns into a pupa. An adult butterfly or moth will emerge from this pupa.

Strong silk
Hanging by a thread, a delicate pupa looks like an easy meal to a hungry animal. But many moth caterpillars spin a cocoon (silken case) to protect the pupa. Most predators cannot break through the strong silk.

Leaflike
This may look like an old wrinkled leaf – but it is really a comma pupa suspended from a twig. It has shiny silver spots that sparkle in the light and make the pupa look empty inside.

The pupa stays very still, but lots of changes are taking place inside the case.

Be careful when you handle pupae – they are very soft and fragile.

Finding pupae
You might see pupae on leaves, twigs, or bark. But you can also find them underground. Caterpillars climb down trees, wriggle through the soil, and hollow out a little space for themselves – where they change into a pupa.

The silken thread, called a girdle, wraps around the caterpillar's body.

The caterpillar shrinks and tightens up as the pupa begins to form under its skin.

Once the pupa skin hits the air, it begins to harden.

Splitting its skin
After the caterpillar of the swallowtail butterfly finds a place to pupate (turn into a pupa), it holds on with its hind legs and spins a silken thread. This strong thread supports the caterpillar while it waits a few hours for its final skin to split.

Empty caterpillar skin

New skin – old skin
The caterpillar has to wriggle around to slip out of its old skin. As the new pupa skin forms, the caterpillar skin falls down to the bottom.

Back legs grip the twig.

Can you see the wings? They are developing inside the pupa.

Final form
The pupa of the swallowtail butterfly can be either green or brown, to match its surroundings. This one looks like a green leaf dangling from a twig. Turn to the next page to see a butterfly hatch from its pupa.

The perfect insect

The final stage in the metamorphosis of a butterfly or moth is very exciting. The insect that emerges from the pupa is very different from the caterpillar that made it. A total transformation has taken place. Keep a lookout for pupae ready to hatch. You will not be disappointed with what follows.

Hatching time

Look for a pupa with a split in it. This is a sure sign that things are about to happen! First the legs and antennae will appear from this split, followed shortly after by the rest of the body.

Split in pupa

Wing patterns are sometimes visible through a pupa that is ready to hatch.

Antennae

Crumpled and soft

Once it has emerged, the wet and delicate insect crawls to a place on the empty pupa from which it can hang downward to dry out.

Wings are crumpled and wet.

Pump, pump

The butterfly pumps blood from its body to the veins in its soft wings. This allows the wings to expand to their full size.

Ready for takeoff

The wings reach full size in about 30 minutes, but they still have to harden. About an hour later, the butterfly is ready to take to the air in search of refreshment. Butterflies do not eat leaves. They drink nectar from their favorite flowers instead.

Once the wings have reached full size, the butterfly opens and closes them until they are completely dry.

Red rain

As the butterfly dries out, waste fluid is squirted from its body. In some species, such as the painted lady, this fluid is red. If a group of butterflies emerge from their pupae at the same time, it looks as though it is raining blood onto the ground below!

Silk cocoons

Moth caterpillars, like those of butterflies, spend the third stage of their metamorphosis as a pupa – and many spin a cocoon to protect them while they pupate. Silkworms – which are not really worms at all, but the caterpillars of the silkmoth – spin a very fine silken thread to make their cocoons with. We use this silky thread to weave delicate clothes.

After hatching, silkmoths live only a few weeks. During this time they mate, and the female lays eggs on her cocoon.

Cosy corner

The silkworm chooses a safe, cosy place to spin its cocoon. This can take up to two days, and the silken thread can be a half-mile long by the time the cocoon is finished.

The silkworm begins to spin a silken thread that comes out through holes under its head.

As the silkworm continues to spin silk, the cocoon gets thicker.

Fussy eaters

Silkworms are very fussy about their food. Only mulberry leaves will do – they would starve rather than eat anything else!

The cocoon is now strong enough to protect the silkworm as it changes into a pupa.

Soft but tough

The pure silk thread produced by silkworms is sometimes used for making parachutes, as well as fine clothes.

Breaking out

Soon after the silkworm has changed into a pupa, it is ready to hatch. To do this, the moth makes a hole at one end of the cocoon by dissolving the threads with a special fluid. As soon as it has crawled out, the moth starts to expand and dry its wings.

You will not find silkmoths in the wild. They are bred only for their silk on special farms.

Sensitive feathery antennae help the male detect a special scent given off by the female moth.

Hole where the moth crawled out

Leave me alone!

Butterflies and moths are very good at letting their enemies know that they do not want to be eaten. Hungry birds, spiders, reptiles, and small mammals are often scared away by aggressive displays. And the bright colors and markings of many butterflies and moths warn predators that they will taste very nasty.

I've got my eye on you!

This fierce-looking owl butterfly frightens its enemies by displaying a large "eye" on its wing. It makes it look more like an angry owl than a delicate insect.

Can you spot the false eye?

Resting on a leaf, this large butterfly could be mistaken for a bird.

Dead smelly

When disturbed, the white ermine moth pretends to be dead. If this does not work, it produces drops of foul-smelling yellow liquid.

Yellow drops warn that the moth is poisonous.

Some harmless butterflies mimic (copy) poisonous ones. The pattern and vivid colors of the monarch butterfly warn birds that it is poisonous. The viceroy butterfly copies its markings to trick hungry birds. Not many will risk a bite to find out which is which!

White spots on the monarch's head and thorax are a signal to predators of the butterfly's awful taste.

The viceroy has a black line on its hind wing. What other differences can you see?

Plant poisons

The monarch caterpillar stores poisons from its food plant – the deadly milkweed – in its body. These poisons are passed on to the butterfly during metamorphosis.

The caterpillar is unharmed by the poisons from its food plant.

Caught in the act

Sometimes false eyes are not enough to protect butterflies and moths from predators. This butterfly was too busy drinking nectar to notice the spider creeping up on it.

False eye

Hide and seek

Not all butterflies and moths are brightly colored to warn enemies that they are poisonous. In fact, most moths – and some butterflies – are very dull in color. These insects have found another way of protecting themselves. Just like caterpillars, these adults use camouflage to hide from birds and reptiles. This lets them blend in with the shapes, patterns, and colors of trees, rocks, or leaves.

The patterns and colors of the moth's wings help it blend in with the tree trunk.

Bark blender
Birds would have a hard job finding this little moth from tropical rain forests. It is quite safe resting on the tree trunk – as long as it keeps still.

Master of disguise

Can you find the butterfly resting in these leaves? Perfect in shape and color, this leaf shoemaker butterfly blends in completely with the leaves it copies. Imagine how difficult it would be for a bird to find!

Veins on butterfly wings look just like veins on leaves.

Moth detective

Finding camouflaged moths can be very difficult. But with a little detective work, you may spot some. Search on tree trunks, posts, or fences for camouflaged moths. See how many you can find, but try not to disturb them.

Broken twigs?

The shape and color of these mating buff tip moths make them look like broken twigs on a tree. As long as they stay still, they are safe from enemies searching for a meal.

Light-colored marks on wingtips look like the broken end of a twig.

Escaping the weather

On a cold day, you might feel like staying in bed or moving somewhere that is warm and sunny. Just like you, butterflies and moths try to avoid the cold. Some hibernate: this means finding a sheltered spot and spending the winter asleep. Others form huge groups and fly to warmer places to escape the cold. This movement is called migration.

North America

Mexico

Follow the arrows to see the monarchs' route.

South America

Large wings help monarchs fly long distances without tiring.

Monarchs stop at flowers to refuel on sugary nectar.

Sun seekers

The monarch migrates more than any other butterfly on Earth. Groups of thousands fly south to spend the winter in the mountain forests of Mexico and southern California. They return north in the spring.

Millions of monarchs

Migrating monarchs rest together on pine trees high up in the mountains. Sometimes they are covered with snow for many days. If you stayed outside for so long you would die, but a chemical in the butterflies' blood stops them from freezing to death.

Masses of hanging butterflies cover the tree for several months.

European painted ladies fly over high alpine mountains.

Flying fan

The painted lady is one of the hardiest butterflies in the world – it can travel up to 600 miles.

1000

Bogong pit stop

If you live in Australia, watch out for migrating bogong moths. They can cover the walls of buildings as they rest on their journey south. The moths will spend the hot dry months in caves in the Australian alps.

Gray and black coloring on underside camouflages hibernating butterflies.

Don't disturb hibernating butterflies and moths – they could die!

Just hanging around

Peacock butterflies hang upside down when they hibernate. Look for them in garden sheds, hollow trees, and even inside houses. They do not eat or move for six months until the spring.

In the garden

Filled with colorful sweet-smelling flowers, gardens attract lots of butterflies by day and moths at night. In the summer, you'll see caterpillars attacking leaves, moths hiding in tree bark, and butterflies sunbathing on flowers. During the winter, a few of these insects seek shelter indoors – but they may come out for a visit on warm days.

Ragged wings
The comma butterfly is a master of disguise – its ragged wings make it look just like an old brown leaf.

This hawthorn leaf is a good place for the moth to lay its eggs.

Garden guest
The brimstone moth is a familiar garden visitor. It hides by day, but it may come out to find a new resting spot. At dusk, look for the moth flying around the lights of houses.

Attracting butterflies

By choosing plants that caterpillars like to eat, you can attract butterflies into your garden. Try planting some nettles in a sunny spot by a wall or corner. How many different butterflies can you spot?

Wear gloves when planting nettles – they can sting!

Silver-spotted skipper

If your garden has lots of colorful flowers, you might see some silver-spotted skippers fluttering about. Look for the silver spots on the underside of their wings.

These butterflies rest with their antennae forward and wings back.

Fast feeders

Elephant hawkmoth caterpillars eat plenty of leaves and flowers during their short lives. They do much of their feeding at night but may eat garden plants such as fuchsias during the day. If disturbed, they swell up the front of their body like a big balloon.

Skeleton leaves

Peacock, red admiral, and comma butterflies all lay their eggs on nettle leaves. The caterpillars eat so much that they make the nettles look like skeletons.

Red admiral resting in the sunshine

The peacock butterfly shows off its false eyes as it flies away.

In the woodlands

Woodlands are one of the best places to look for butterflies and moths. You'll find butterflies fluttering on flowers in sunny glades or resting on twigs and branches, and moths hiding in leaf litter on the ground. Look out for caterpillars feeding on leaves and plants – some extra-hungry moth caterpillars cause a lot of damage by stripping the leaves from trees.

The silver-washed fritillary sunbathes with its orange-spotted wings open.

Top of the tree

On hot summer days, look for purple hairstreaks and silver-washed fritillaries near oak trees. They stay in the canopy (top of the tree) when it is sunny, but also sunbathe on oak leaves near paths and clearings when it is warm.

The purple hairstreak's shiny wings change color in the sun.

Fun in the sun

Like most butterflies, the heath fritillary loves the sun. It hardly moves in dull weather, but comes out to sunbathe in sunny woodland glades when it is hot. It lays its eggs on plantain.

What is the longest thread you can see on a spring woodland walk?

The dull-colored pine processionary moth blends in well with the bark of pine trees.

Dangling from danger

The oak leaf roller caterpillar lives inside a rolled-up leaf. When ants threaten, it throws itself off the leaf and dangles on a silk thread it has spun. When the coast is clear, the caterpillar crawls back up the thread onto the leaf, just like a mountaineer climbing up a rope.

Processionary caterpillars can damage pine woods by stripping trees of their needles.

Follow the leader

Pine processionary caterpillars set off in a line to look for food – the front caterpillar spins a thread of silk that the others follow. After they have separated and eaten, the caterpillars fall into line again and follow the thread of silk back to the nest.

On the edge

The eggfly butterfly can be spotted in many different places, including Australia and North America. It only lives on sunny woodland edges and clearings – you'll find it visiting wild and garden flowers, such as lantanas and zinnias, to sip nectar.

In the mountains

Walk through a mountain meadow in the summer, and you'll find it alive with butterflies and moths. But mountain weather changes quickly. Dark clouds, snow flurries, and high winds can come in minutes – and insects at the top have to work hard to adapt to these sudden weather changes.

High and low

Most predators won't touch the poisonous monarch butterfly, so you'll find it in the lowlands as well as on mountain tops.

Greasy wings

The small apollo butterfly has a special survival feature for life in the mountains. Its greasy wings help it survive freezing weather, including sudden snow flurries.

Dark spots trap the sun's heat.

Thick hairs keep the insect warm.

Look for the small apollo on high mountains in Europe and Asia.

Look for three long tails on the hind wing.

When harsh winds blow, the scarce copper holds on tight.

Mountain glory

The Bhutan (*boo-tan*) glory butterfly lives in the mountains of India and Thailand. The tails on the insect's wings are important. Predators see these first and peck them – leaving the more important parts of the insect alone.

Tough moth

Nothing is hardier than a burnet moth. Look for this red and black survivor in the mountains of Central America, Asia, and Europe. It tastes so bad that birds spit it out immediately, leaving large numbers of caterpillars and moths to survive and breed.

Warm and windy

Many mountain insects survive the cold winter by sunbathing during the day. But strong winds can turn a sunny day into a windy nightmare. This butterfly clings to a rock to avoid being blown away.

In the rain forest

No other place in the world has as many colorful butterflies and moths as the tropical rain forest. Lots of rainfall and a variety of plants make rain forests an ideal home for these insects. The best places to spot butterflies and moths are in sunny places by riverbanks, in clearings, and around flowers.

Butterfly-shaped wings glitter in the sunshine.

You can tell this not a butterfly by the antennae – they have no clubs at the tips.

Butterfly or moth?
It looks like a butterfly, and flies by day like a butterfly, but it's really a moth. This uranid moth lives in the Amazon rain forest in South America.

This nero butterfly sticks its proboscis into the damp sand to find water.

Water seekers
Male butterflies have to drink lots of water that is rich in salts. They need these salts to make special scents for attracting mates. Every few seconds, they squirt out any excess water.

Two-headed caterpillar

In the rain forest, you may spot a caterpillar that looks like it has two heads. Its back end has a horn and a funny face to confuse birds and lizards – they never know which end to attack.

Delicate wing patterns help to camouflage this butterfly.

Invisible wings

Glass wing butterflies are very hard to spot – their see-through wings make them look invisible. This disguise works so well that some moths have copied it.

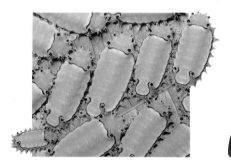

Safety in numbers

Lots of rain forest caterpillars live in groups. The bigger the group, the safer they are. These limacodid (*lee-ma-co-did*) caterpillars are brightly colored and covered with poisonous spines – so predators keep their distance.

Flashy flier

Look for this flashy malachite (*mal-ah-kite*) butterfly flying around the open areas of a rain forest. It loves to visit flowers and drink their sweet nectar.

In the desert

You may not see many butterflies or moths flying around the desert in the middle of the day. Most of them seek shelter to avoid the heat of the midday sun. The best time to watch for butterflies and moths is in the morning or the evening. Look for them flying around water holes where grasses and wild flowers grow.

A long wait
A butterfly waits for the rain to fall before emerging from its pupa. In the hot, dry desert, this can take several years.

The gray-brown color makes this butterfly invisible in the sandy desert.

A smelly drink
For butterflies and moths to survive on the dry plains of Africa, they have to find water every day. This African ringlet even drinks from animal droppings!

The butterfly's shortened proboscis helps it to puncture tough plants.

Yucca feeders

After hatching, caterpillars of the yucca skipper butterfly tie the leaves of the yucca plant together with silk. They feed inside the leaves, safely hidden from predators. Later they eat inside the plant and bore into its roots.

Look for caterpillars feeding on the leaves of yucca plants.

Escaping the heat

Flying in the early morning sun, and again in the cool of the evening, this little tiger blue butterfly escapes the scorching desert sun. At midday it rests under a rock and keeps very still, so it does not get exhausted from the heat.

Phantom of the desert

As the sun sets in the Australian desert, look for the large ghost moth flying about in search of food and water. Its light colors and long wings make it look just like a scary phantom.

The shiny spots on the front wings reflect the sunlight and keep enemies away.

In the Arctic

It would be very difficult for us to withstand the freezing winters, strong winds, and short summers of the Arctic. But a few butterflies and moths live there all year round. They have special survival features, such as antifreeze in their blood and dark colors to absorb heat quickly.

Summer flier
This Arctic clouded yellow butterfly flies when the sun is shining. As soon as the clouds come out, it seeks shelter. A special liquid in its blood keeps it from freezing – just like the antifreeze in a car's radiator.

Cocoon in the cold
When temperatures fall below zero, Arctic pupae remain safe inside protective silk cocoons.

The long hairs on its body help keep the butterfly warm.

Catching rays

To make the most out of the weak Arctic sunshine, the sooty ringlet stretches its wings across a warm rock and lifts its body in the air.

Dark colors and heat already trapped in the rock keep the butterfly warm.

Summer feast

You'll find lots of butterflies visiting flowers during the short Arctic summer. Butterflies depend on flowers for sugary nectar. But they must be careful – many hungry birds and spiders are waiting nearby.

The speckled pattern of the Arctic fritillary helps it hide from its enemies.

At rest on a rock

Most Arctic moths spend their nights making low, short flights from flower to flower. They have to hide by day, to avoid being eaten. This moth stays perfectly still on a rock, relying on its camouflage to pass undetected.

Index

Eyed hawkmoth

*Swallowtail
butterfly*

*Butterfly
emerging
from its
pupa*

Red underwing moth

Puss moth caterpillar

Catepillar with false head

Acknowledgments

Dorling Kindersley would like to thank:
Sharon Grant and Wilfrid Wood for design assistance.
Michele Lynch for editorial assistance and research.
Linda Martin for editorial work on initial stages of book.
Jane Parker for the index.

Illustrations by:
Brian Hargreaves, Nick Hewetson, Tommy Swahn

Picture credits
t=top b=bottom c=center l=left r=right
Jane Burton: 10.
Matthew Chattle: 14tl.
Steve Gorton: 9bl, 15.
Dave King: 49tr.
Kim Taylor: 30-31blr.
Bruce Coleman Ltd: 51bl; /J. Brackenbury 16tl; /M. Fogden 55cl; /Jeff Foott 47tl; /D. Green 32l; /Jan van de Kam 37t, 37tr, 37bl; /L.C. Marigo 33br; /Sandro Prato 41b; /Frieder Sauer 52c; /John Shaw 52t; /Kim Taylor 27tr, 45b; /Peter Ward 31tl, 61.
Oxford Scientific Films: /Mantis Wildlife Films: 25t.
Planet Earth: Alan Barnes 19tr; /A. Kerstich 30tl; /Mary Sherdian: 36b.
Premaphotos: 27tl, 44, 45c, 48tl, 55tr.
Wildlife Matters: 42c.